Interreligious Prayer

Interreligious Prayer

A CHRISTIAN GUIDE

THOMAS RYAN, CSP

Paulist Press
New York/Mahwah, NJ

Cover design by Sharyn Banks
Book design by Lynn Else

Library of Congress Cataloging-in-Publication Data

Ryan, Thomas, 1961–
    Interreligious prayer : a Christian guide / Thomas Ryan.
       p. cm.
    Includes bibliographical references.
    ISBN 978-0-8091-4513-3 (alk. paper)
    1. Prayer. 2. Prayer—Christianity. 3. Christianity and other religions.
I. Title.
    BL560.R93 2008
    204′.3—dc22

                                                   2007044707

Published by Paulist Press
997 Macarthur Boulevard
Mahwah, New Jersey 07430

www.paulistpress.com

Printed and bound in the
United States of America

Contents

Acknowledgments vii

Introduction..1

1. Biblical Perspectives 5
    Exclusivist Perspectives...5
    Inclusivist Perspectives...6
    The Dialogue between God and Humankind.................8
    Hospitality 9

2. Reflections on Prayer and Worship...............................13
    How Do You Understand "God"? 13
    What Is the Basis for Coming Together to Pray?..........14
    Christian Prayer as Covenant, Communion,
        and Gift...16
    Does Interreligious Prayer Negate Our
        Commitment to Witness?...18
    Are There Any Boundaries in Interreligious
        Worship and Prayer ?...20

3. Different Forms of Interreligious Prayer 22
    Just Being There...23
    Multireligious Prayer...23
    Integrative Religious Prayer...28
    Leadership of Prayer at a Multifaith Gathering 38

CONTENTS

4. Practical Considerations 41
    Preparation 41
    Respect for Forms Employed 42
    Theme 43
    Site 43
    Day and Time 44
    Order and Content 44
    Language 45
    Holy Writings 45
    Symbols and Rituals 45
    Music and Singing 46
    Silence and Meditation 46
    Food and Drink 46

5. Final Reflections 47

6. Appendix: Some Resources 51
    Judaism 51
    Christianity 56
    Islam 61
    Hinduism 65
    Buddhism 68
    Sikhism 73
    Baha'i 75
    Native American 77

Notes 79

Acknowledgments

This project began with an invitation from the Connecticut Christian Council of Churches to write guidelines for interreligious prayer that would provide helpful radar and landing gear by which to touch down on the increasingly frequent occasions wherein people from different religious communities come together to pray. The early draft I wrote, which they took as a serviceable instrument for their needs, proved to be but a working document for me that would continue to evolve and grow, benefiting from the experience, wisdom, and input of many.

The members of the Faiths in the World Committee of the U.S. Catholic Association of Diocesan Ecumenical and Interreligious Officers were generous in their time in reviewing the text and offering helpful suggestions and recommendations. My sincere thanks to Ecumenical and Interreligious Affairs officers Sr. Josephine Kase (Philadelphia), Rev. Philip Latronico (Newark), Ms. Judith A. Longdin (Milwaukee), and Rev. Francis Mazur (Buffalo); to committee members Rev. Thomas Baima at the University of St. Mary's of the Lake (Mundelein, Illinois), Professor Donald Mitchell (Purdue University), Rev. John Pawlikowski (University of Chicago), and Rev. Francis Tiso at the U.S. Catholic Bishops' Conference.

Other colleagues with long experience in the field of interfaith relations also provided helpful comments and feedback, most notably Archbishop Michael Fitzgerald, papal nuncio to Cairo and delegate to the League of Arab States; Dr. John Borelli and Rev. Leo Lefebure at Georgetown University; and the executive director of the Monastic Interreligious Dialogue, Rev. William Skudlarek, OSB.

These perspectives and guidelines, while having no official and formal approval, carry the wisdom, insight, and experience of many. They are, however, a work in progress, and will continue to benefit from the deepening relationships between people of faith and from a growing reservoir of communal experience. They are offered in the conviction that, at some point, it makes sense to assemble what we have learned thus far and move forward, guided by a coherent integration of the wisdom and insight presently available.

My deep gratitude and expression of thanks to all those who have contributed from their experience and learning.

Thomas Ryan, CSP

Introduction

Participation in interreligious prayer is not an optional activity restricted to an elite group, but an urgent call for a growing number of Christians today, and should be a matter of concern for all Christians. In the pluralistic world in which we live, concrete situations of everyday life provide opportunities for encounter with people of living faiths. These include interfaith marriages, personal friendship, praying together for a common cause (in the context of war, racism, human rights violations, AIDS, etc.), national holidays, religious festivals, school assemblies, meetings between monastic communities of different faiths and gatherings at interreligious dialogue centers.[1]

So spoke a group of twenty-five participants from a variety of Christian traditions and from different parts of the world in a consultation on interreligious prayer arranged jointly by the Office on Interreligious Relations of the World Council of Churches (OIRR) and the Vatican Pontifical Council for Interreligious Dialogue (PCID).

While recognizing that the development of interreligious prayer will be related to particular situations, the members of the consultation encouraged the churches to joyfully respond to the new opportunities of not only meeting and working with members of other religions, but also, where appropriate, praying with them. "We believe," they said, "that such prayer is a symbol of hope, which both reminds us of God's purpose and promise for justice and peace for all people and calls us to offer ourselves to be used in this work."[2]

Their words signal a new awareness of the enormous potential religions have for the healing of the world, if only the spiritual energies they represent can be harnessed. When Christians and people of other religious traditions lived separated from one another in well-defined geographical locations, the situation of interreligious prayer was not a reality to contend with.

But that has changed, and certain pastoral questions now arise: Do we need interreligious prayer? Could it enhance our spiritual lives? Or might it divert and mislead us from the true worship of God in spirit and in truth? What pastoral assistance should we offer to the increasing number of people who find themselves in situations of interreligious prayer? Interreligious prayer has become a serious issue for which there is no easy answer.

While the situations giving rise to interreligious prayer may not yet be a reality for most Christians, we do well to give careful consideration to both the caveats and the positive reasons for it. We will find ourselves looking for compass bearings to guide our steps.

Our need to explore these questions is not just a matter of expediency resulting from religious communities increasingly being thrown together because of population movements. Rather, the imperative flows out of a recognition that prayer is the shortest way between humans because God is the One who is nearest to us. Prayer is the strongest bond because it goes through God. In our distressed, broken world, prayer is a bond of peace. Can we afford to ignore the opportunities we have for it?

It is, in fact, faithfulness to the Gospel that impels us now to re-examine our attitudes toward other religions and their adherents. The opportunity to take into greater consideration what we have in common and what requires us to live our destiny together is a grace of our time.[3] Thus the Catholic Bishops' Conference of India, in its "Guidelines for Interreligious Dialogue," presented prayer in common with members of other religions as not only possible, but recommended—a duty, even.

> The purpose of such common prayer is primarily the corporate worship of the God of all who has created us to be one large family. We are called to worship God not only individually but also in community, and since in a very real and fundamental manner we are one with the whole of humanity, it is not only our right but our duty to worship him together with others.[4]

The document makes clear that discernment and preparation are required, and it explains that pastoral judgments must be made as to what is possible and advisable. But it also is clear that, generally speaking, common prayer between Christians and members of other religions is both possible and desirable in the context of contemporary interreligious dialogue.

Various situations, however, must keep in mind the religions involved, the concrete circumstances, and the choice of prayers that can be sincerely shared among the different participants.

In saying as much, it should be recognized from the outset that these reflections are enunciated from a Christian perspective, and that monotheistic assumptions about prayer are not shared by all religious traditions. Buddhists, for example, sometimes feel that monotheists assume all religions are in some way theistic and worry that their own approach is then misunderstood.

It must be respectfully acknowledged that there are different assumptions at work in any planning group looking at the possibility of interreligious prayer. The desire here is simply to offer Christian participants some guidelines consistent with their own faith. It is understood that should representatives of

Buddhism or Hinduism or any other religious tradition undertake a similar project of guidelines for their adherents, that they would also do so from their own perspectives.

Those studying the development of the religious life of humankind are convinced that as a human family we are on the threshold of a new corporate consciousness of being a global community. We are being pushed to a stage in which every religious person has been opened to the possibility of learning from all the religious traditions.[5] The groaning of the Holy Spirit within our hearts until all things are made full is being experienced in new ways.

Biblical Perspectives

In the Bible there are what the theology of religions today identifies as "exclusivist" and "inclusivist" perspectives. A religion that adopts an exclusivist perspective believes that its way alone saves people and that other religions do not lead to salvation.

In an inclusivist understanding, a particular religion would hold that the divinity, as it understands it, is present and at work in all religions and is moving them toward itself without their being fully aware of who it is that is leading them. By virtue of this inner divine direction, the other religions derive their power to save. What the other religions offer only vaguely, beneath obscure symbols and even in part misrepresented, will gradually be purified as they are led by their most profound inner longing toward their proper essence. We will briefly look at some examples of both exclusivist and inclusivist approaches to people of other faiths in the Bible.

EXCLUSIVIST PERSPECTIVES

Many biblical passages reflect the belief that God supported Israel, whereas other nations were to be hated and destroyed. In Israel's settlement in the promised land, for example, the people are instructed to destroy the places of worship of the Canaanite religions (Num 33:52). According to Deuteronomy, the statutes and laws given to the people required them to "break down [the Canaanites'] altars, smash their pillars, burn their sacred poles with fire, and hew down the idols of their gods, and thus blot out their name from their places" (Deut 12:3). Even though Israel assimilated and accommodated many elements from the cultures and religions that surrounded her, the worship of alien deities in its many forms is uncompromisingly forbidden (Isa 40:18–10; Jer 10:1–9; Wis 13:10—14:31).[1] This struggle of the prophets against "the worship of idols" goes on unabated throughout the history of Israel down to the times of the Book of Daniel and the Maccabees, who will die rather than worship idols.

Most forms of popular religiosity in the ancient civilizations both of the Middle East and of the Greco-Roman world were really forms of base idolatry mingled with superstition and even immoral practices. The "pedagogical" reason for this relentless crying out against the worship of idols is intended to bring Israel to a deeper knowledge of God in view of its special mission. Yet we cannot just dismiss it as a historically conditioned phenomenon. It is an important part of the biblical message. Thus, the covenant on Mount Sinai is seen clearly as a separation from the other peoples in view of a purification and consecration for a special encounter with God and a form of worship that God will reveal to Israel (Exod 19—31; Deut 12—16).[2]

Both testaments of the Bible warn against worship that encourages idolatry and harms human dignity. Addressed first of all to Israel concerning its own worship, this warning calls all of us to act with prudence, discernment, and courage in resisting forms of worship and prayer that corrupt God's image and are harmful to society's moral and social fabric.[3]

INCLUSIVIST PERSPECTIVES

Over against exclusivist trends in the Bible, one also finds strong affirmations of openness to other faiths and cultures.

Worship offered to the Lord by people who are not Jews is acceptable to God (Dan 4:34–37; 6:25–27; Isa 19:16–25). Those who are not Jews are required only to recognize Yahweh as the true Lord and are not obliged to convert. For example, in the story of Jonah—a bold affirmation of God's concern for all peoples, not just Israel—Jethro, Nebuchadnezzar, and the people of Nineveh remain within their own cultural and religious traditions. These are people who, like Melchizedek and Balaam, are represented as raising their hearts in prayer to God, who responds to them. The story of Naaman the Syrian (2 Kgs 5:17–19) also suggests tolerance toward other religious traditions. The prophet Malachi appears to say that all worship reaches the one God: "People from one end of the world to the other honor me [says the Lord]. Everywhere they burn incense to me and offer acceptable sacrifices" (Mal 1:11, Good News Translation). The teaching of the great prophets of the Old Testament led people away from a tribalistic approach to an inclusive and universal outlook.[4]

In the New Testament, Jesus was confronted by exclusivist traditions of the Pharisees and Sadducees. Whenever there was an opportunity, he drew attention to the impressive faith of others. He praised the faith of the Roman centurion (Matt 8:10; Luke 7:9) and the Syrophoenician woman (Matt 15:21–28; Mark 7:24–30), and told the Jews that they could learn from the Samaritans (Luke 17:11–19). His approach was that, rather than making exclusive claims for our own faith, we should be appreciative of what is good in other people's faith: "Many will come from east and west to sit with Abraham, Isaac and Jacob at the banquet in the kingdom of heaven" (Matt 8:11).[5]

The biblical evidence for inclusiveness, however, is not overwhelming, and it would be inappropriate to build arguments based on selected texts. But what is overwhelming is the affirmation that God is one and that God cares for all people. The psalms are unequivocal in claiming "that the earth is the LORD's and all who dwell in it."

THE DIALOGUE BETWEEN GOD AND HUMANKIND

From Adam and Eve onward, the Bible is clear that God desired to enter into dialogue with all human beings. Even after Adam and Eve broke away from God through sin, God spoke with Cain both before and after his terrible crime of killing his brother.

This ongoing encounter with God is the very purpose of creation. This call to dialogue, to communion, continues down the ages and makes of the whole of human history an uninterrupted dialogue between God and humankind. Human beings are instructed and raised by God, like a child by its father and mother, to learn to utter the name of God, to talk to God, to *pray.* This dialogue between God and human beings reaches its highest and most intimate expression in Christ.[6]

There is no doubt in the writers of the New Testament that this dialogue between God and humankind reaches a new and consummate level in God's manifestation in Jesus. Through him the Word of God is made flesh and dwells among us (John 1:14). Through him we have access to the Father in the Spirit (Heb 4:14–16). We can give a new and fuller answer to his call and speak to him as the Spirit teaches us to do (Rom 8:15). Jesus asks us to pray "in his name" (John 14:13–14; 16:24–27), that is, with him, and through him, and in him. He teaches us to call God *Abba* (Matt 6:9; Luke 11:12) through the Spirit of adoption that he pours forth on us (John 7:39; 14:16; 15:26). So the church, faithful to his teaching, addresses her official prayer to the Father, through the Son, in the Holy Spirit.[7]

How we understand the plurality of religions in the economy of God's salvation will greatly affect and influence our understanding of interreligious prayer. God's covenants with Noah and with his descendants and with every living creature that was with him (Gen 9:9–17), with Abraham and his offspring for an everlasting covenant (Gen 17:1–7), with Moses and the descendants of Jacob to make of them a living symbol for the salvation of the whole human race (Exod 24:3–11)—these covenants remain valid forever, testimonies to God's dialogue with humanity throughout the ages. They are not abolished, but come to full flower in God's covenant with "the nations" in Jesus, his anointed one. The previous covenants and the religious expressions of them retain, for the peoples concerned, their salvific value and role and should be recognized, respected, and appreciated as such by Christians.[8]

We then acknowledge with gratitude to God that the peoples of the world have their covenant with God from the beginning, and their religious expressions of fidelity to it, just as they have their own "prophets." And the descendants of Abraham have a special covenant by virtue of their special election by God, who said to Abraham, "I have made you the ancestor of a multitude of nations" (Gen 17:5). All this is part of the one and only history of salvation and is attributed by the Bible to God's own initiative and to his covenants with humankind.[9]

At the same time, in Jesus we recognize God's never-to-be-surpassed revelation to humankind and the mediator of our salvation.

HOSPITALITY

Hospitality is an essential component of the biblical tradition. The word *hospitality* derives from *hospes,* meaning both "guest" and "host." It implies mutuality. Biblical literature develops the theme of the close relationship between God and the stranger or sojourner. In the patriarchal stories of the Hebrew Scriptures, we find Abraham and Sarah offering hospitality to three strangers by the oaks of Mamre (Gen 18:1–15), Lot providing a feast and lodging to two angels in Sodom (19:1–11), and Rebecca's brother Laban taking in Abraham's servant (24:14–61).

In some biblical stories, God is identified as both guest and gracious host who befriends the Israelite people while they were strangers. In other stories, like those concerning Melchizedek (Gen 14:18) or the people of Nineveh (Jonah 3:1–10), God shows acceptance of those of other nations who seek to walk in holiness.

In the New Testament as well, Jesus is identified as both guest and host. He remains a wayfarer who depends on the hospitality of others (Matt 8:20; Mark 7:24; Luke 7:36; John 12:12). He is the supreme host when he washes the feet of his guests and breaks bread for them to eat (Mark 6:41–45; Luke 22:27; John 13:1–17). To act hospitably is the criterion Jesus gives to his followers for positive judgment before God (Matt 25:32–42). For Jesus, "neighbor" is coextensive with "humanity" to such an extent that the stranger becomes the neighbor, as in the story of the Good Samaritan showing true compassion for a Jew (Luke 10:29–37), in spite of tensions between Jews and Samaritans.[10]

When Jesus sends his disciples to announce the kingdom of God, he instructs them to first ask and receive hospitality (Luke 10:7–8). It is an exchange. One will both receive and give. The many occasions that are given to us today to meet people of other races and religions are a chance to live this teaching of Christ. Christians, and the Israelites before them, have always received much from others—their culture, their philosophy, even elements of their religion—but without daring to acknowledge this, as if what we offer would be thereby diminished. The time has come to "rejoice in the truth": our receiving as well as our giving has been an occasion for mutual enrichment.[11]

Christian hospitality, manifesting the hospitality of the kingdom of God, extends to all peoples. Dispositions for hospitality include a willingness to listen to the needs of the world, to acknowledge a preference for the poor and the stranger, and to maintain an openness that is conditioned by humility and kindness, and a readiness to meet and be with the other.

The rationale for interreligious events is grounded in the gospel imperative to love, to serve, to be with in solidarity, and to affirm our neighbor, and to attend to the work of God throughout the *oikumene,* the whole inhabited earth. A consultation arranged jointly by the Office on Interreligious Relations for the World Council of Churches and the Pontifical Council for Interreligious Dialogue offers some theological reflections on this gospel imperative that invite us to see how interreligious prayer can be a way of practicing love toward the neighbor and tending together to the needs of the world:

> In the Bible we meet God as creator of the whole world, a God of justice, mercy, love, and peace in the midst of the vicissitudes of life. We meet Jesus Christ as the Son of God reconciling humankind with the Father and human beings among themselves. We meet the Holy Spirit as the Giver and Sustainer of Life, the very source of prayer and intercession....
>
> God is love. The love for God and the love for our neighbor cannot be separated....Interreligious prayer can be seen as one way of practicing love towards our neighbors and of striving with them in a common effort to build a more peaceful and just world.
>
> Listening attentively to the word of God, we discover in it at least two ways of speaking about prayer in other religious traditions. The Bible teaches us that God, out of His goodness, has spoken with human beings and made with them covenants from the very beginning and down the ages of human history. Through tradition from the early beginnings of the Church, we learn about several covenants, with Adam and Eve before the flood, in the time of Noah after the

flood, in the time of Moses with the gift of the Law, and finally the covenant in Christ which brings humankind into a new closeness with God.

The Bible also speaks about human beings responding to God with prayers and sacrifices which are pleasing to God, as in the stories of Abel, Noah, and Melchizedek. In such authentic prayer, Christians can recognize the working of the Holy Spirit. Also, the biblical tradition of sacred hospitality should encourage us to a genuine openness towards people of other religions.[12]

Everywhere and at all times we are all guests of the Divine, and whatever we do to or with our neighbor, we do to or with the Divine (Matt 25:31–45). God in Christ both goes before us and comes to us in the guise of our neighbor and the stranger in our midst.[13]

Is our sharing with one another limited to food and drink, or might it upon occasion be extended to prayer? We will now look at some of the expected and accepted limits and parameters within which authentic engagement at this level can occur with mutual integrity.

2

Reflections on
Prayer and Worship

HOW DO YOU UNDERSTAND "GOD"?

Prayer is the universal aspect of religion. It is to religion what rational thought is to philosophy. Even though every human being may not engage consciously in prayer, it is a natural, normal, and inalienable part of being human to have an instinctive feel for what prayer is, especially in moments when the human heart is confronted with the finitude of human existence or elevated by the mystery of life. Prayer is an act by human beings to be in communication with the sacred, the holy, the other, or in common parlance, God.[1]

But the subject of interreligious prayer raises a series of important questions. Who, or what, is God? Are we all praying to one and the same God even if our images and understandings of God are different? Doesn't the distinction between an image of God as a person and an impersonal mysticism of identity affect the essentials, even if all concepts and images fall short of the ineffable reality of the absolute?

These questions illustrate the complexity between coming together in prayer with monotheists who have a personal concept of God and with religionists whose concept is either impersonal or nontheistic. In Buddhism, for example, the word *prayer*

---

is used analogously to its usage in theistic traditions because Buddhists do not pray to a transcendent God.

Given the biblical perspectives we have considered flowing from revelation, the personal nature of God is indispensable for Christians and is an inalienable gift. There is a difference between praying to a God who sees and hears, recognizes and stands over against you, and intentionally "oneing" yourself with an infinite being with which you are already identified at your deepest level and into which you wish to be absorbed.

The whole Christian mystical tradition of apophatic prayer[2] notwithstanding, leaving behind the belief in God as a "person" has implications that should not be ignored: God no longer sees me, hears me, speaks to me. Because perceiving and willing are the two essential elements in the concept of person, there is no will of God. Neither is there any ultimate distinction between good and evil; they no longer stand in contradiction but merely in a relational opposition of complementarity. Between a personal and an impersonal concept of God, there is no middle way. Consequently, praying, in the case of an impersonal understanding of God, obviously means something quite different from praying in faith to one personal God.[3]

WHAT IS THE BASIS FOR COMING TOGETHER TO PRAY?

If there is, then, a real difference in our prayer, what is the basis for coming together to pray?

When Pope John Paul II invited representatives from other churches and world religions to come to Assisi, Italy, in 1986 for a day of prayer for peace, he offered this rationale:

> The coming together of so many religious leaders to pray is in itself an invitation today to the world to become

aware that there exists another dimension of peace and another way of promoting it which is not a result of negotiations, political compromises, or economic bargainings. It is the result of prayer, which, in the diversity of religions, expresses a relationship with a supreme power that surpasses our human capacities alone....

The fact that we have come here does not imply any intention of seeking a religious consensus among ourselves or of negotiating our faith convictions. Neither does it mean that religions can be reconciled at the level of a common commitment in an earthly project which would surpass them all. Nor is it a concession to relativism in religious beliefs, because every human being must sincerely follow his or her upright conscience with the intention of seeking and obeying the truth.

Our meeting attests only—and this is its real significance for the people of our time—that in the great battle for peace, humanity, in its very diversity, must draw from its deepest and most vivifying sources where its conscience is formed and upon which is founded the moral action of all people....

Peace, where it exists, is always extremely fragile. It is threatened in so many ways and with such unforeseeable consequences that we must endeavor to provide it with secure foundations. Without in any way denying the need for the many human resources which maintain and strengthen peace, we are here because we are sure that, above and beyond such measures, we need prayer—intense, humble, and trusting prayer—if the world is finally to become a place of true and permanent peace....

Religions are many and varied, and they reflect the desire of men and women down through the ages to enter into a relationship with the Absolute Being. Prayer entails conversion of heart on our part. It means deepening our sense of the ultimate Reality. This is the very reason for our coming together in this place.[4]

The Second Vatican Council's declaration *Nostra Aetate* (*Declaration of the Relationship of the Church to Non-Christian Religions*) addressed the common origin of the entire human race in God through creation and our common destiny in God through the mystery of redemption. In speaking to the Roman Curia about the interreligious event held at Assisi, Italy, in 1986, John Paul II further developed this theme, noting that the differences between us in the human family—whether of skin color, geography, or culture—are "less important than the unity, which by contrast, is radical, basic, and decisive."[5]

The foundational groundwork for our coming together to pray, then, lays in our radical unity of origin, destination, and incorporation into the same divine plan for every human being who comes into this world. Another theological foundation for interreligious prayer can be added to this: the universality of the reign of God, in which Christians and others are co-participants. As such, we are also co-creators of the reign under God, called to promote justice and peace, faith and charity, freedom and dignity of all God's children. It takes but a moment's reflection to recognize that God's reign will only come about through the active collaboration of people of every religion working together in response to God's grace and call.

CHRISTIAN PRAYER AS COVENANT, COMMUNION, AND GIFT

Additional foundational stones for interreligious prayer flow from the nature of Christian prayer as demonstrated by the experience of covenant, communion, and gift. Can these characteristics be shown to be inclusive of the prayers of members of other religions as well?

Christian prayer arises from a covenant relationship between God and us in Christ. God entered into covenants with Noah, Abraham, Moses, and their descendants; those who walk with an upright and pure heart in these covenants thus walk with God. In God's indefectible covenant with every living creature, God calls all people to prayer.[6]

A second mark of authentic prayer is communion. Here, prayer can be understood in the simplest of terms: presence responding to Presence. Contemplative prayer in Christian understanding is living with a conscious awareness of God's presence, available to us always and everywhere by virtue of our baptismal union with God in Christ and through the Holy Spirit. This deep communion in the life of God binds Christian believers together in what has sometimes been called a "mystical body."

As we have noted, however, the Holy Spirit is literally a "free spirit," a wind that "blows where it wills" (John 3:8). The Second Vatican Council (1962–65) recognized the Holy Spirit's activity outside the visible body of the church and of "all people of good will in whose hearts grace works in an unseen way. For, since Christ died for all, and since the ultimate vocation of man is in fact one and divine, we ought to believe that the Holy Spirit in a manner known only to God offers to everyone the possibility of being associated with the paschal mystery."[7]

Thirdly, prayer is a gift of the Holy Spirit. Many churches today have acknowledged the presence of the Holy Spirit in other religions and cultures, but nowhere is that theme more frequently addressed than in the writings of Pope John Paul II.

In his various texts, a constant teaching emerges: the universal presence and activity of the Holy Spirit is recognized not only in Christians, but also in members of other religious traditions. For example, in his encyclical *Dominum et Vivificantem*

(The Lord and Giver of Life), he writes that the action of the Spirit "has been exercised in every place and at every time, indeed in every individual."[8]

In his encyclical *Redemptoris Missio (The Mission of the Redeemer)*, John Paul II expresses his conviction that "the Spirit's presence and activity affect not only individuals but also society and history, peoples, cultures and religions."[9]

If that is so, can the prayers of people in other religions also be gifts of the Holy Spirit? Can the same Spirit be active in the hearts of those who pray them? "We may think," writes John Paul II, "that any authentic prayer is aroused by the Holy Spirit, who is mysteriously present in the heart of every human being."[10] This mysterious communion, born of the Spirit's presence, is available to all.

He sees even the "firm belief" of the followers of other religions as "an effect of the Spirit of truth operating outside the visible confines of the Mystical Body."[11]

Interreligious prayer, then, may well express our being united in the Holy Spirit, a coming into the presence of God *together*, even if this *together* is in a limited way in our understanding.[12]

This, then, is the basis for our coming together to pray: creation, redemption, the universal presence and activity of the Holy Spirit, joint sharing in the reign of God, and the Christian understanding of prayer anchored in the experience of gift, covenant, and communion.

DOES INTERRELIGIOUS PRAYER NEGATE OUR COMMITMENT TO WITNESS?

Prayer is the yearning of the heart for communion with God. We are incurably religious. The urge to pray wells up from deep within us in response to the mystery of life and creation that surrounds us. It is a uniquely human activity that transcends the boundaries of race, culture, and creed.[13]

However, to the extent that prayer is also a confession of faith and an explicit doxology, it is generally not possible to borrow the formulations that define another faith. But if one considers the movement of prayer—the groaning of the Holy Spirit in the heart of everyone who prays, or the praise that comes to the lips of every believer—this engagement in prayer can indeed be lived with the faithful of other religions. Christ, instead of excluding those who did not conform with the norms of his religion, such as the Roman centurion or the Canaanite woman, saw inside their hearts and marveled at their way of expressing their trust in God.

Our participation in interreligious prayer does not negate our commitment to witness. As Cardinal Ratzinger, later Pope Benedict XVI, wrote in *Truth and Tolerance: Christian Belief and World Religions:*

> The question of truth plays a part in the relations between religions, and that truth is a gift for everyone and alienates no one....If in Christ a new gift, the essential gift—truth—is being granted us, then it is our duty to offer this to others, freely, of course, for truth cannot operate otherwise, nor can love exist.[14]

What role does truth play in the relations between religions? The Pontifical Council for Interreligious Dialogue's (PCID) document *The Attitude of the Church Towards the Followers of Other Religions* describes dialogue as a process in which Christians and people of other religious traditions "walk together toward truth."[15]

Christians instinctively might respond, "Wait a minute! Didn't Jesus say 'I am the Way, the Truth, and the Life?' And if that's so, how can we who believe in Christ still be walking together toward truth?" The PCID's response is:

The fullness of truth received in Jesus Christ does not give individual Christians the guarantee that they have grasped that truth fully. In the last analysis, truth is not a thing we possess, but a Person by whom we must allow ourselves to be possessed. This is an unending process. While keeping their identity intact, Christians must be prepared to learn and receive from and through others the positive values of their traditions.[16]

Truth is a gift for everyone and alienates no one. Members of all religions are called to offer their understanding of it to others.

Praying together is one of the ways in which we witness our belief in the central truth of God's love for all, and in the Holy Spirit's presence and work in all. Our prayer with people of other faiths expresses our desire to overcome barriers and prejudices toward one another and to promote the life that Jesus brings to the world.[17]

In our prayer with members of other religions, there inevitably will be an implicit invitation to them to discover the communion with the Triune God that we have begun to enjoy. Such a witnessing dimension also will be present on the part of those with whom we join in prayer. Finding the riches of God's grace in the others and their spiritual tradition can itself be cause for joy and hope and lead us to praise and thanksgiving.[18]

ARE THERE ANY BOUNDARIES IN INTERRELIGIOUS WORSHIP AND PRAYER?

Worship generally does not refer to an individual's quest for communion with the divine, but to an ordered response to a realized experience of the sacred within a specific community.

As such, it by and large refers to the acts of communities and takes the form of adoration, praise, thanksgiving, and petition.[19] *Liturgy* is an organized ritual function to enable the participation of adherents.

Worshiping communities often have a central event, a story, which is their window on the divine. For the Jewish community it is the revelation of the Torah on Mount Sinai; for Christians it is both the revelation of the Torah and Jesus' life, death, and resurrection; for Muslims it is the revelation of the Qur'an. In each community, worship is built on a story that is celebrated in narratives, symbols, and rituals, which are largely meaningful only to those who share the story.[20]

It is difficult to maintain a clear distinction between prayer and worship because prayer is what people understand themselves to be doing in the context of worship. But what can be helpful in finding our way with interreligious prayer is the distinction between the story that is internal to the life of a particular community and places where prayer can open to others and find common ground.

The internal story is our private space, the place wherein we derive a distinctive identity. Within this inner circle, each community has its core liturgical life and celebrates its story. Those who do not share this story may be allowed to be observers and engage to a certain extent, but they will not participate fully because it is the community's space. Thus it is that non-Hindus generally are not allowed into the inner sanctum of the great temples of India, that non-Muslims do not get into the line at daily prayer, that non-Jews would not proclaim from the Torah in the synagogue, and that non-Christians do not receive at the table of the Lord's Supper.

Beyond this space, however, there is a realm that we might call the commonwealth of human ritual gestures.

3

Different Forms of Interreligious Prayer

The commonwealth of human ritual gestures offers a wide range of practices, symbols, values, rituals, and forms of prayer that recur in most religions and can be employed in interreligious prayer. When one or more of these are used, some may feel a certain kinship with it out of their own experience. Examples of what the commonwealth of human ritual gestures holds include: prayer postures; bowing; prostrations; silence; meditation; fasting; sharing of food and hospitality; music; poetry; dance; processions; bells; incense; flowers; Peace Pole; search for Truth; the Golden Rule; pilgrimage; commitment to moral living, justice, and peace; acknowledgment of wrongdoing and the need of forgiveness.

Interreligious prayer is an expression of the coming together of all the "scattered children of God" and hopefully leads to a more united and peaceful human family. In his call to world religious leaders for a day of prayer at Assisi in 1986, Pope John Paul II identified some of these common ritual gestures when he observed, "This day is, therefore, a day of prayer and for what goes together with prayer: silence, pilgrimage, and fasting."[1]

Prayer together is an invitation to friendship and a sign of the unity of humanity. It presupposes an attitude of respect, a willingness to learn from and be enriched by the faith expression of other religious traditions. It is a response to the mystery whose name cannot be limited to a single name and whose action on behalf of humanity is not entirely contained in any single narrative.

Here are possible scenarios.

JUST BEING THERE

Attendance at the formal prayer rituals of another faith community makes a positive statement all of its own. The demonstration of simple respect and high regard between members of once-estranged faiths is an important religious value in itself. Simple presence is also a form of participation.

Example: At the Monastic Interreligious Dialogue (Catholic–Buddhist) Gethsemani Encounters,[2] Buddhist monks were present respectfully as observers for the praying of the psalms in the Divine Office and for the celebration of the Eucharist. Similarly, Catholic monks attended the daily Buddhist rituals.

MULTIRELIGIOUS PRAYER

This refers to a service or occasion in which prayers of different faith communities are juxtaposed or presented in serial fashion. It describes a situation in which people come together in full fidelity to their own faith and offer an expression of it while at the same time opening their hearts with sincere respect and interest to the faith expressions of the others. When representatives of the world's religions gathered in Assisi, Italy, in 1986, they followed the formula: "We come together to pray rather than come to pray together." Pope John Paul II described what they would do in these words:

> We shall go from here to our separate places of prayer.
> Each religion will have the time and opportunity to

express itself in its own traditional rite. Then from these separate places of prayer, we will walk in silence towards the lower Square of Saint Francis. Once gathered in the square, again each religion will be able to present its own prayer, one after the other. Having thus prayed separately, we shall meditate in silence on our own responsibility to work for peace. We shall then declare symbolically our commitment to peace.[3]

In multireligious prayer, representatives of one faith community offer their prayer while the other participants listen in reverent silence. They place themselves as "participant observers." They know they do not pray that way, but they are willing to stand by that brother or sister in a mode of solidarity. This does not imply acceptance of everything that is said or done, nor does it suggest indifference to truth.

There is a strong resonance between multireligious prayer and interreligious dialogue. Both involve, on the one hand, respectful attention to the expression of another religious tradition's faith-experience, and, on the other hand, witnessing to what Christian faith is. Dialogue is giving and receiving, listening to and speaking with others, recognizing what God has worked in their hearts, and witnessing to what God has done in our own lives.[4]

Every religious tradition has its own characteristic way of praying that expresses its identity and self-understanding. In multireligious prayer, we discover what is proper and unique in other religious traditions, appreciating all that is good, beautiful, true, and useful in order to know God better and to love God more. At the same time, we witness to our faith and the reason for our hope, as well as sharing with them the service of our love and the source of our joy.[5]

Example: During One World Week in England, prayers were offered by members of various faith communities. A Muslim chanted the Sura Hashar from the Holy Qur'an. A Buddhist led a litany of peace, punctuated by moments of silence. A Hindu chanted the Gayatri mantra. A Sikh offered a recited prayer. A Christian sang the "Our Father." The service closed with an international prayer for peace.

Example: An Observance for Commonwealth Day in England featured meditative readings from the scriptures of different traditions on themes of universal concern:

- Stewardship of the earth: A chanting of Surah 56 from the Qur'an.
- Human worth: A reading from the Mishnah Sanhedrin.
- Justice and peace: Readings from the Sikh Guru Granth Sahib and a Baha'i reading from The Hidden Words of Baha'ullah.
- Love in relationships: A reading from the Buddhist Sutta-Nipata from the Discourse on Loving-Kindness.
- Service and sacrifice: A reading from the Gospel according to St. Luke.

The service also involved a procession, meditation, bells, interpretative dance, and music.

Example: An interfaith service took place in Alumni Arena in Buffalo, New York, on the occasion of the Dalai Lama's visit. The following is an outline of the ceremony:

- Welcome (master of ceremonies).
- Musical prelude (Tibetan flute master).
- Procession (Dignitaries from the religious communities are welcomed by a delegation of the Haudensaunee, the first people to settle in western New York.).
- Readings, prayers, and chants from sacred texts, with responsive gestures from students in the University of Buffalo's Department of Theatre and Dance:

~ Native American passage from John Fire Lame Deer (Lakota).
~ Baha'i prayer by 'Abdu'l-Bahá.
~ Jewish contemporary song: "Peace may yet come to us."
~ Christian "Prayer of Peace" from Saint Francis of Assisi.
~ Muslim verse from the Qur'an (49:13).
~ Sikh commentary on the Guru Granth Sahib by Saran Singh.
~ Hindu traditional prayer for peace.
~ Buddhist traditional chant, the Metta Sutta.
~ Unitarian Universalist poem, "The Oversoul," by Ralph Waldo Emerson.

- An address to the assembly by His Holiness the Dalai Lama.
- Reflective silence, initiated by the striking of the keisu, a Japanese monastic bell.
- Responsive reading (an antiphonal litany-style arrangement). For example:

  One: May we act upon what we have heard and said, with intention and determination, with sincerity and prayer.

  All: We are peace, we make peace.

- Breaking down borders with keepsake strings. As a gesture of mutuality and good faith, participants tie on one another's wrist a string enclosed in their order of service.
- Recessional (choral performance by a local choir).

Example: An interfaith festival of chants was held in Chicago, Illinois, featuring Gregorian chant; Sanskrit and Pali chanting; the Qur'an; Kirtans, Jewish, Zen, and Sufi chants.

While the Chicago festival was multireligious in its approach, many are introduced to the experience of integrative or communal chanting through the increasingly popular practice of yoga. It is now estimated that there are some eighteen million Americans who practice yoga, many of whom are Christian. It is a common experience for yoga practitioners to find themselves at a weekend or evening program that features a kirtan or the singing of *bhajans* (devotional chants). Often, the chants are in Sanskrit, so it is not always clear what one is singing. At other times, loose translations are provided. Not all chants are devotional in nature; sometimes one might be invited to chant simple "seed-syllables" for harmonizing one's inner energies. But devotional chants frequently address or invoke Hindu deities.

A common explanation offered by way of reassurance to those who find themselves feeling ambivalent is that there is just one Supreme Being of all religions (Saguna Brahman), and the various deities actually represent different aspects or attributes (*sagunas*) of the one Supreme Being.

The problem for Christians, as well as for Jews and Muslims, is that the saguna forms are venerated as such, that is, as real gods who, when propitiated, grant specific requests or bestow certain graces. It is the act of worship that is problematic. The veneration of the deity forms runs counter to the first commandment in the Decalogue: "I am the Lord your God. You shall have no other gods before me" (Exod 20:2).

Intellectually, one can respect the high-level Hindu belief that saguna deities are just manifestations of the one Supreme Being. But words, like *deity* and *worship*, and the understandings behind them, matter. If they did not, Muslims would feel free to pray the "Our Father," which in general they decline to do, and Christians would think nothing of getting in the prayer line with Muslims, which they generally do not do, to make their profession of faith that "there is no god but God and Mohammed is his prophet." Similarly, tantric Buddhist practitioners will avoid expressing heartfelt adoration in devotional chants to the saguna manifestations because it violates the root tantric commitment of not venerating or invoking "worldly deities."

Generally, when Christians pray with Hindus in India, they employ chants that use generic names like God, Lord, or Creator that can be applied to the God of one's own understanding, but beyond that they do not use actual names. Religious traditions generally recognize that there is an energy around the specific names for deities, and when we invoke those names with heartfelt devotion, those energies do not remain without but in some sense enter in.

Thus the counsel: one should not enter into that energy field without being formally initiated to it. Christians have been initiated in baptism into the Body of Christ, into the love energies of God revealed as Jesus-Emmanuel (God-with-us) whose Holy Spirit has been poured out into our hearts. So chant those names. Intensify those divine energies within you.

For many, multireligious prayer is the best course. Each group respects entirely the ritual prayer of the other faiths while maintaining a reverent attentiveness and without trying to participate directly in them. While multireligious prayer will not be the normal form of religious life for any of the involved communities, in special circumstances it serves as a poignant expression of our co-partnership as servants of and participants in extending the reign of God in our world.

INTEGRATIVE RELIGIOUS PRAYER

Here the intention is not simply to come together to pray, with each group or delegation offering prayer in accord with its own prayer tradition, but to actually pray together. It is not uncommon to encounter Christians, or members of other religions, too, for that matter, who are skeptical as to whether this is even possible or who see it as reductionist or syncretistic and thus to be avoided.

Syncretism in this context is understood as an uncritical amalgam. Reductionism refers to how the prayer forms, of necessity, do not highlight the distinctiveness of the beliefs in the various religions and require foregoing some of the typical expressions of faith characteristic of those traditions (e.g., for Christians, ending a prayer with the Trinitarian formula) so that other believers can actively join in. Thus, integrative religious prayer can give rise to hesitation or controversy in a way that multireligious prayer does not. It is worthwhile giving clear expression to these concerns.

For some, prayer together is only possible if there is agreement on who or what God is and on what praying is (e.g., a process of dialogue in which I talk to a God who is able to hear and take notice). The fundamental agreement also extends to the content of the prayer, that is, to what it is worthwhile to pray for. There is a desire to avoid giving the impression that the basics of Christian belief are not of ultimate significance and thus replaceable. In this view, if a Christian's participation were seen by non-Christian participants as the relativizing of faith in Jesus Christ as the Savior of all, then that participation could not be recommended because it would be pointing backward instead of forward in the history of the way to God.[6]

While these concerns are real, there are nevertheless Christians, particularly in countries where Christianity is a minority, who have engaged in integrative religious prayer and who continue to explore this frontier. From their experience, several considerations are offered.

Distinction between Prophetic and Mystical Religions

In order for a prayer to be shared by members of diverse communities of faith, there must be sensitive pastoral discernment that takes into account the theological relationship among the communities involved, the doctrinal content of the prayer, the place where the prayer is said, and any gestures that may accompany it. It should be recognized that a universal prayer will be said with different "accents" and understandings as each community present prays it in accordance with its own faith. Such variations, however, will retain a common irreducible substrate on which is grounded the validity of sharing in prayer.[7]

In terms of the theological relationship among the religions involved, the distinction between the three monotheistic or prophetic religions and the mystical religions of the East may be helpful. These terms of identification are not intended to deny that Asian religions can turn to an absolute who is also personal or can have a prophetic dimension; nor are they meant to deny to the monotheistic religions a mystical dimension. The point is simply to recognize that the three so-called monotheistic religions go back to a common historical origin in the faith of Abraham and thus belong to a common family. All three unequivocally claim to be rooted in the God of Abraham, and common prayer among them can be seen as a concrete embodiment of Abrahamic hospitality.[8]

While this does not mean that all three religions have the same notion of God, it does recognize a common historic foundation that opens up broader alternatives for Jews, Christians, and Muslims who come together in prayer. The sacred scriptures of the various traditions offer several possibilities, such as the psalms of the Hebrew Bible; the prayer of Jesus (the "Our Father"), whose content and wording are deeply inspired by the spirituality of the Hebrew Bible; the *fatiha,* the Sura that opens the Qur'an by way of invocation of Allah (see appendix for all three).

In all three prophetic religions, both prayer that is prescribed by the regulations of worship and spontaneous prayer have developed many methods and styles. Nevertheless, for the three religions, prayer has the same deep meaning—worship of God and identification with God's will—in spite of the differences that they have in their approaches to the divine mystery. Members of all three communities organize their lives around the practice of regular prayer whereby, through invocation and thanksgiving, they integrate their work, their joys, and their sorrows into their prayer. Jews, Christians, and Muslims, by means of their regular cycle of prayers and festivals, make all the important stages of human experience from birth to death the focus for praise and thanksgiving, for supplication and prayers for forgiveness. Thus, it is mutually enriching for members of these faith communities to learn more from one another about how they respectively "sanctify life" through prayer.[9]

What Pope Benedict XVI said to Muslims in his visit to Turkey in 2006 applies as well to Jews and underscores the importance of strengthening our relationships with one another through all possible means:

> Christians and Muslims belong to the family of those who believe in the one God and who, according to their respective traditions, trace their ancestry to Abraham.
>
> This human and spiritual unity in our origins and our destiny impels us to seek a common path as we play our part in the quest for fundamental values so characteristic of the people of our time. As men and women of religion, we are challenged by the widespread longing for justice, development, solidarity, freedom, security, peace, defense of life, protection of the environment and of the resources of the earth....[We] have a specific contribution to offer in the search for proper solutions to these pressing questions.
>
> ...We are called to work together, so as to help society to open itself to the transcendent, giving Almighty God his rightful place. The best way forward is via authentic dialogue between Christians and Muslims, based on truth and inspired by a sincere wish to know one another better, respecting dif-

ferences and recognizing what we have in common. This will lead to an authentic respect for the responsible choices that each person makes, especially those pertaining to fundamental values and to personal religious convictions....

May we come to know one another better, strengthening the bonds of affection between us in our common wish to live together in harmony, peace and mutual trust. As believers, we draw from our prayer the strength that is needed to overcome all traces of prejudice and to bear joint witness to our firm faith in God.[10]

When members of one or all the Abraham religions come to pray together with members of the so-called Eastern mystical religions, additional discernments are called for. Whereas theistic currents are quite widespread in Hinduism, in Buddhism those currents are nontheistic. With Buddhists, a viable way forward is a time for common meditation in silence.

As was noted earlier, members of the different communities will inevitably enter into the time of prayer with the understandings that characterize their own beliefs. Whenever people open up in faith and entrust themselves to an absolute on whom they depend completely, it is natural for Christians to interpret that reality in terms of the universal presence and self-manifestation of the God revealed in Jesus Christ. While it is true that the prayer of Christians is "to the Father through Jesus Christ in the Holy Spirit," it is also true that this is not always given explicit expression in every prayer Christians pray even among themselves.

For some Christians, then, this opens the possibility that Christians and people of other religions, in spite of their conceptual differences about the divine absolute, can together address their prayer or meditation toward that absolute who in any case is beyond adequate mental representation. Mindful of the active presence of the Holy Spirit in every sincere prayer, the prayers offered together are seen to simply make it possible for all to meet in the Spirit of God, present and at work in the hearts and lives of all.[11]

In short, despite the deep doctrinal differences between Christianity and the Eastern mystical religions, there remains a shared theological substrate (common origin through creation and destiny through redemption, universal activity of the Holy Spirit, joint sharing in the reign of God) and an anticipated communion, which is destined to grow through the practice of dialogue and can be expressed uniquely in common prayer and contemplation.[12]

Some Lines of Approach

A. Resources from the commonwealth of human ritual gestures may be employed, or prayer resources of a more generic nature either drawn from each tradition or not belonging exactly to any particular religious tradition but accepted by all. While this form of prayer may be useful at times and even may be the only one possible, it does not by itself bring out the richness within the traditions as fully as multireligious prayer, though the range of possibilities is greater than one might think.

Example: A service could include an invocation from Native Americans, a song led by Christians that all are invited to sing, a reading from the Qur'an, a chant for peace led by Buddhists and a prayer led by a Jew (in both of which all are invited to participate), and a blessing offered by a Hindu.

B. The integrative approach to prayer may also pertain when there are just members of two or three different faith communities together. When Jews and Christians join in prayer, or members of the three Abrahamic religions (Jews, Christians, and

Muslims) come together, there is a greater possibility of using biblical texts because Jews and Christians share the Old Testament or Hebrew Scriptures (albeit with some different interpretations), and the Qur'an includes many references to persons and episodes of the Hebrew and Christian scriptures.

Example: Representatives of the Jewish, Christian, and Muslim communities in Dallas, Texas, selected seventeen psalms of thanksgiving and praise for use by the children of Abraham. The particular psalms selected: 1, 19, 23, 31, 34, 37, 46, 57, 63, 92, 100, 103, 112, 113, 127, 141, 145.[13]

The ninety-nine names of God in Islam are also beautiful and rich and represent another potential resource for "coming to pray together" (see appendix).

Example: In a year when the Muslim month of Ramadan coincided with both the Jewish high holy days and the feast of St. Francis of Assisi, a group of Christians, Jews, and Muslims came together in New York City "to celebrate [their] traditions and heed God's call to seek peace and pursue justice." The event began with presentations by a representative from each faith community on "Our Sacred Texts: Ways to Peace or Ways to Violence?" This was followed by a time of integrative prayer, after which participants shared an evening meal together. The components in the time of prayer:

> Call to prayer.
> A prayer for peace (prayed by all):
>> O God, you are the source of life and peace. Praised be your name forever. We know it is you who turn our minds to thoughts of peace. Hear our prayers in this time of war. Your power changes hearts. Muslims, Christians, Jews remember, and profoundly affirm, that they are followers of the one God, children of Abraham, brothers and sisters. Enemies begin to speak to one another. Those who were estranged join hands in friend-

ship. Nations seek the way of peace together. Strengthen our resolve to give witness to these truths by the way we live. Give to us understanding that puts an end to strife; mercy that quenches hatred; and forgiveness that overcomes vengeance. Empower all people to live in your law of love. Amen.

Penitential rite.

Readings from sacred scripture:

Micah 4:1–4

Matthew 5:1–12

Sura II, v. 136; Sura VIII, v. 61; Sura XXV, v. 63; Sura XLIX, v. 13

Silent meditation.

Litany (of the following nature):

Leader: Do we commit ourselves to building peace in our families, in our communities, in our countries, and among the nations of the world?

All: We do.

Final blessings.

C. It is possible to include multireligious and integrative religious prayer elements within one service. In other words, the time of prayer may contain moments when representatives from one tradition offer prayers distinctive to their own faith, and within the same service there may be symbolic actions, songs, or prayers that unite all the participants. Thus there may be a going back and forth between distinctive and unitive prayers and actions.

Example: Shortly after September 11, a multireligious service of prayer took place in St. Paul's Church next to Ground Zero. At end of the service, all present went outside and gathered on the newly constructed viewing platform. The Buddhists led the various religious representatives in chants for peace in English. Similarly, at the end of the post-September 11 multireligious service at Yankee Stadium, all present sang together the prayer ascribed to St. Francis, "Make Me a Channel of Your Peace."

Example: A service bringing together Jews, Christians, and Muslims at Merrimack College in North Andover, Massachusetts, opened with the Muslim Call to Prayer, called by an imamma (female imam) who then recited the Al-Fatiha, the opening chapter of the Qur'an, which stands in approximately the same relation to Muslims as the Lord's Prayer does to Christians.

A rabbi, Catholic priest, and imamma then led prayers of peace, love, and brother/sisterhood from their respective traditions, each accompanied by a three-minute discourse on these themes. The Merrimack Music Ministry sang *Dona Nobis Pacem* (Mozart) with Hebrew translation.

After commenting on the rituals of washing and blessing of bread in their respective traditions, the leaders then invited participants to wash each other's hands and, after blessing some bread, passed it among the attendees while the choir sang.

A Jewish cantor introduced and sang *Shalom Aleinu/ Salaam* (composed by Jews and Muslims), inviting everyone to sing (transliterated lyrics provided in program).

The imamma gave a final Muslim blessing to conclude the time of prayer.

When the multireligious approach is combined selectively with the integrative approach through the juxtaposition or mingling of different ritual elements, confusion may be created in the minds of some participants. A challenge for planners is to arrange things so that no impression is given that the religions and their beliefs are interchangeable. Procedures such as these are exceptional and should be characterized by a careful explanation, both for those present and those who will simply hear about it, of what is and is not happening.

As we have seen, integrative religious prayer contains within it some calculated trade-offs, such as sacrificing the full particularity and distinctiveness of each tradition for the sake of general harmony and for the desired benefit of engaging in prayer together. It is worth pointing out in this context that we do not always use the highest forms of prayer available in our traditions. There are circumstances that call for simple prayers, almost spontaneous invocations.

The following is an example of the kind of prayer that might find expression in a service characterized by integrative prayer:

> O Ancient Mystery, ever new, bring wisdom and guidance to all those who walk on many paths to the same source.
> You who are called both Mother and Father of Creation, strengthen those who work for the protection and safety of all life—animal, mineral, plant, human, spirit—that our world and cosmos may breathe in security and exult in its manifold beauty.
> You who are the Source of our peace, unite families in love. Root out violence and crime from our midst. Defend those who are abused. Restore the rights of the deprived. Let world leaders provide justice for the needy, and bring a swift end to all wars and oppressions.
> O Living Source of Life and Light, ever shining in glory, deepen the faith of the wavering. Console the sorrowing. Let those who wander find a path of truth. Give health to the sick, fortitude to the distressed, and may people of all religions live in one fellowship of harmony and work together for one world of tranquility.

Pastoral leaders who work the frontier of our new pluralist reality may upon occasion decide that, given the important or tragic nature of the events that bring them together, some compromises are worth making for the sake of common prayer and the impetus it provides toward deeper conversion to God on the part of all the participants or partners in dialogue. However, they should not be naïve to the fact that even when one has the best intentions, there can be unintended negative consequences from something as simple as saying prayers from other traditions.

Example: A Christian minister in the United States once began a Eucharist with the characteristic Muslim profession: "There is no god but God." An Iraqi student in the congregation was highly indignant because he understood that line to deny the Christian faith in the Trinity.

Similarly, when the "Our Father" was discussed in the Midwest Dialogue of Catholics and Muslims, the Muslims said they did not wish to say the prayer because to Muslims the term *Father* has Trinitarian overtones.

These examples make clear that there is no substitute for joint planning and discussion among representatives of the different communities that will be taking part in the service. It is in such meetings that questions can be clarified and the best choices discerned. Obviously, integrative prayer requires all participants to show a great sensitivity and a deep respect for both the differences and commonalities existing between the various religious traditions.

As communities grow together in relationship and confidence, there may be a corresponding desire in exceptional circumstances not just to observe silently each other's ways of praying, but to explore ways of praying together.

LEADERSHIP OF PRAYER AT A MULTIFAITH GATHERING

For leaders of an invocation that opens the community to the divine presence on occasions such as a university convocation ceremony, a Thanksgiving Day service, or an interfaith wedding, the key question is "Am I praying on behalf of everyone?" If so, it will be appropriate to forego the particular expression of one's own faith so that all present will be able to feel themselves represented and included in the prayer offered on their behalf. It will be necessary to use a language that is both intelligible to and inclusive of all the persons present. Sensitivity toward all the participants is the guiding principle.

Example: Asked to offer an interreligious benediction at Emory University during a ceremony to welcome the new president of the university, the chaplain prayed:

> As a new chapter opens, a new flower blooms, and a fresh fragrance of novelty and expectation spreads,
> Let us step into the future with confidence and hope.
> May our pursuit of excellence be complemented by our desire to care for each other!
> May our search after truth be accompanied by our appreciation of plurality and variety!
> May our works of beauty be sensitized by the ugly realities of suffering and pain!
> And may our acts of goodness be tempered by a deep sense of humility and grace!
> The One, the One who is called by many names and yet meets us as the nameless One,
> That One, may that One surround us, sustain us!
> Let it be so, let it be so! Amen.[14]

The final statement from a Bose international meeting encouraged all Christians to seek to ensure that a practice intended to promote human unity does not become a cause of division. "We recognize," the participants said, "that Christians may sincerely disagree about what is appropriate." They thus recommended that Christians exercise discernment in the light of their faith in Christ when they participate in multireligious and integrative prayer.[15]

Interreligious prayer may not be a vocation for most Christians, and surely those who are called need careful formation and a deep prayer life of their own. But we must all consider the positive reasons for the various modalities of interreligious prayer as described above and prayerfully discern the appropriate time and place for each one, whether it be just being there, multireligious, or integrative religious prayer. For if the Holy Spirit is in it and behind it, then those Christians involved in interreligious prayer may be following Christ in ways that we have only come to dimly fathom. We shall know them by their fruits.[16]

4

Practical Considerations

PREPARATION

A collaborative approach is essential in planning. If it is not planned interreligiously, it is not an interreligious event. A service planned by one group with others invited is a service sponsored by the former with the latter as their guests.

Interreligious ceremonies grow out of and reflect respect for all traditions present. This respect should find expression in collaboration in the planning as well as in the actual event. It is helpful to ask: What is the conceptual framework of worship for the others with whom I will be worshiping? The tendency for Christians, understandably, is to operate out of a Christian template for worship and to want to organize the components of other religions accordingly in the service.

While prayer is a universal phenomenon, it encompasses a diversity of religious expressions. No particular structure for interreligious services is required. Great variety among as well as within services is to be expected, as interreligious prayer relates to particular situations and should be shaped by those involved. Keep in mind that people want to look up in a service and at some point see someone who looks like them, and hear something that sounds familiar.

There is a rationale for a multireligious service, an integrative service, and for an admixture of elements from both. Be prepared to give an account of your rationale for the approach chosen.

RESPECT FOR FORMS EMPLOYED

While one of the enrichments of interreligious prayer is the opportunity to enter into the prayer-experience of the other, respect must be given to the uniqueness of prayers emanating from other traditions as well. Some Buddhists, for example, do at times use the word *prayer* with reference to Tibetan prayer wheels and prayer flags or in chanting to Guan Yin, but this is not prayer to a transcendent God.

Some Buddhists would also want to keep a distinction between their nontheistic meditation and a Christian's appropriation of it into a theistic framework. Both within and outside the service, our appropriation of the religious symbols and prayer methods of others should respect the integrity of the other and use sensitively what we have found to be of value without conveying a sense of "co-opting" or "taking over" the other's tradition.

An example of such co-opting would be a Christian adaptation of the Seder by interspersing or concluding it with New Testament readings or Christian associations, or turning it into a Eucharist or a prologue to a Eucharist. Such mergings would show a lack of respect for Judaism and a distortion of both Christian and Jewish traditions.

Showing respect for a form employed might result, on the other hand, in a demonstration Seder arranged in cooperation with a local synagogue and led by a Jew to assist the Christians present to understand its ritual and meaning to the Jewish community. In all events, Christians should take every care to ensure that the correct Jewish ritual is followed and that the Seder is respected in its full integrity.

The prayers and prayer forms of any one religious tradition are not simply variants of a common species, although they may in themselves communicate meaning and insight that go beyond their own religious context.[1]

THEME

In composing the service, it can be helpful to choose a theme—suggested, perhaps, by a particular event or a shared need—so that the choice of prayers and readings is not haphazard but resonant with one another.

SITE[2]

Many people prefer to be in a place not connected with any particular faith when coming together to pray or praying together, yet a secular venue can cause difficulties for others in establishing a viable setting for worship or in creating a suitable environment.

If the service takes place in a sacred worship space, participants should be informed before they arrive about dress requirements such as head coverings or shawls, whether they are to remove their shoes before entering, where they are required to sit, or which room they are to use. Some seminars in advance of the event might be helpful in explaining the worship space and the purpose of certain dress decorum.

If official representatives of the different religious communities are invited, determine how their seating will be arranged. Are they all to sit on the same level? Take into account that some people feel they need to sit on the floor, while others prefer chairs. Some like to kneel while others would rather stand. Some like to express their devotion in bodily movements or face a particular geographic direction, while others like to sit still and quiet. These are things that should be discussed in the planning stage so that everyone can accept the arrangements that are eventually made.

The size of the gathering also makes a significant difference. Doing something for thirty people who have a relationship with one another allows for much more flexibility than a televised event for thousands.

DAY AND TIME

Unless there is a good reason to build the service around a regularly scheduled ritual in one particular faith community, it is better to avoid having it at a time when any of the participants would normally be having their own principal devotions. Avoid scheduling a multireligious event on a high holiday in the calendar of any of the participating groups.

ORDER AND CONTENT

A printed order of service is recommended because the content and sequence of the celebration most likely will be unfamiliar to many of the participants. It might also include guidance as to what the participants can expect to happen, and what they may be encouraged to do, with alternatives indicated, such as standing, sitting, or kneeling. Those preparing the event should communicate clearly the amount of time allowed for each contribution to those who are invited to lead the different parts of the service. The service may include a welcome and invitation to prayer. Islam has a particular form for the call to prayer that may be useful.

Planners might consider providing some commentary in the order of service on the rationale behind the kind of service chosen, and invite all to pray as they are comfortable or to the extent that they wish.

LANGUAGE

Translations should be provided for any prayers, readings, or mantras that may be read or chanted in the language in which they were originally written. This will enable everyone present to know and appreciate their meaning as well as support their participation.

HOLY WRITINGS

The treatment, handling, and position of the sacred scriptures are important parts of worship within some faith communities. Care should be taken to see that they are duly reverenced and handled only by those authorized to do so. In some traditions it is required that the holy writings be placed in elevated positions.

SYMBOLS AND RITUALS

For historical, theological, and personal reasons, some symbols may be offensive to a particular group participating in a multifaith service. If the symbol is part of the actual architecture of the building (e.g., a fixed cross or crucifix that is part of the worship space), this is acceptable, but it would be more appropriate to lead a procession with a banner or common symbol like fire, water, or incense, rather than a cross.

Symbols that people hold in common, such as light and water, can be an uplifting part of shared prayer (see chapter 3). A careful discernment is called for when using rituals, because they often express the beliefs of one particular faith community that cannot in sincerity be shared by others, therefore limiting participation in them.

MUSIC AND SINGING

Many Muslims would not wish to sing during a service and some would be hesitant about the use of music although these are integral parts of prayer for many faith communities. If Muslims are a participating community, they should be consulted on the appropriateness of the arrangements in this respect.

SILENCE AND MEDITATION

Just being together in creative silence can unite hearts in prayer and lead to a profound sense of unity. The use of quiet and meditation will depend to a large extent, however, on the size and inclinations of the participating group and on the occasion. Whereas many interfaith groups have developed the practice of having a period of silent prayer at the beginning of their meetings, long periods of silence would probably be inappropriate during a large civic service. There are also those who feel uncomfortable with prolonged silence because their cultures express and experience spiritual depth through song and movement. Those preparing the service should consider how much time should be allowed for silence and for meditation, guided or otherwise, and those leading it directed accordingly.

FOOD AND DRINK

For many the sharing of food and drink is a continuation of the relationship engendered by prayer. Those preparing the refreshments should assure that the dietary regulations of different faith communities be catered for and, if necessary, that the foods be clearly labeled so that their contents are known. Similarly, bottled water or fruit juices should be provided for those who do not drink tea, coffee, or alcoholic beverages.

5

Final Reflections

The spread of Christianity through missions both Catholic and Protestant in the eighteenth, nineteenth, and even first half of the twentieth century was often characterized by ignorance of other religions. The attitude of many missionaries with regard to other belief systems was ill-formed and based on a simplistic assumption of the finality, absoluteness, and uniqueness of the faith they held. Today, living in a global village requires a courageous rereading of our history. We are both witnesses and actors in this revolution.

We need to develop a new way of looking at the multifaith context in which we live, seeing it as a part of the richness of the God-given reality. We are struggling to articulate a theology that celebrates our interreligious prayers as a way of reveling in the multicolored, multilayered manifestations of God.

Variety and diversity, reflected in the flora and fauna, are inherent in creation. Similarly, the diversity of religious faith and expression contributes to the beauty and richness of the complex spirituality of the human family. Accepting the legitimacy of different religions is crucial for the quality of our corporate existence and a precondition for peace and communal harmony among us as people of different faiths.[1]

Those who come together for interreligious prayer recognize God's saving presence in each religious community, irrespective of the symbols expressing it. The meaningfulness of interreligious prayer depends on this recognition. Interaction among members of different religions through the dialogue of life, of action, of theological exchange, and of religious experience contributes to mutual learning, correction, and enrichment. It moves us all toward the fulfillment of our common humanity. In a multireligious context, coming together in prayer from time to time is a necessary expression of the human pilgrimage from isolation to communion.[2]

In 1987, the dialogue program of the World Council of Churches, in collaboration with the program on renewal and congregational life, brought together in Kyoto, Japan, about twenty persons from the Protestant, Orthodox, and Roman Catholic traditions who had spent ten years of their lives interfacing with spiritual practices from other religious traditions. The group made three affirmations in its final statement:

> First, we affirm the great value of dialogue at the level of spirituality in coming to know and understand people of other faiths as people of prayer and spiritual practice, as seekers and pilgrims with us, and as partners with us in working for peace and justice.
>
> Second, we affirm the deepening of our own Christian faith in the journeys that have taken us into the spiritual life and practice of other faiths. In walking with the other, with the stranger, like the disciples on the the road to Emmaus, we have had, in our sharing, the experience of recognition. We have seen the unexpected Christ and have been renewed.
>
> Third, we affirm the work of the Spirit in ways that move beyond the Christian compound and across the frontiers of religion and take us into creative involvement with people of other faiths in the struggles of the world.[3]

It is significant that the group did not feel they were being syncretistic in their journeys into the spiritual life and practice of other faiths, but that the Islamic, Buddhist, and Hindu resources with which they came to be familiar enabled them to deepen their own core faith and helped them discover new dimensions of spiritual practice. Their experience has been echoed by that of many others who witness to being strengthened in their own Christian faith and touched by grace in similar situations.

The encounter with meaningful practices in other religions ultimately raises the question about the self-sufficiency of our own faith. Are there areas in which the spiritual life and practices of our own traditions can be enriched and enhanced by interaction with others?

The critical question relative to syncretism is, "What does one do with resources that come from outside one's own tradition, and what effect do they have on the coherence and integrity of one's own faith?" As in everything, so in spiritual practices there is a need for discernment, discrimination, and sometimes rejection. What should be countered, however, is an arbitrary fear of anything that is not "ours."

In an increasingly multifaith society we constantly face situations that call for fresh initiatives and new ways of holding our faith in relationship to others. Isolationism, whether political, religious, or spiritual, can be adopted today only if we are prepared to opt for a narrow, sectarian withdrawal from society.

The dominant motif of Jesus' teaching is love. In announcing the kingdom of God, he brought people an experience of God's love. Extending the reign of God calls us to do likewise, fostering the love of God in all people and promoting solidarity among them. As Pope Benedict XVI noted in conjunction with his first encyclical, *God Is Love,* "A Christian knows when it is time to speak of God, and when it is better to say nothing and let love alone speak."[4]

Jesus' first disciples belonged to a community that had prayed for centuries, but when they were faced with a new reality, they went to Jesus and asked: "Lord, teach us to pray." We may not be asking followers of other religions to teach us to pray, but the new challenge of praying with a wider representation of God's children requires of us today a similar humility and willingness to learn.

In speaking to the woman of Samaria, Jesus indicated that a time would come when "you will worship the Father in spirit and in truth" (John 4:23), a worship not bound to any particular place, be it Mount Gerazim or even Jerusalem, but a worship that consists in offering oneself to God in love and being a sign of God's love to all. Our Christian contribution to interreligious prayer, if it wishes to be faithful to and worthy of the God whom the Bible reveals to us, will strive to be a prayer "made in spirit and in truth."[5]

As such, our interreligious prayer will be a moment of true spiritual experience and commitment, an encounter with God and a service to God's plan of salvation. It will be a feast of peace to which all human beings are invited. It will be a feast of peace in which the disciples of Christ are called, by their faith in him and their baptism in his Spirit, to be the messengers and the servants.[6]

6

Appendix:
Some Resources

JUDAISM

Psalm 150

Praise the LORD!
Praise God in his sanctuary;
   praise him in his mighty firmament!
Praise him for his mighty deeds;
   praise him according to his surpassing greatness!
Praise him with trumpet sound;
   praise him with lute and harp!
Praise him with tambourine and dance;
   praise him with strings and pipe!
Praise him with clanging cymbals;
   praise him with loud clashing cymbals!
Let everything that breathes praise the LORD!
Praise the LORD!

Psalm 121

I lift up my eyes to the hills—
   from where will my help come?

My help comes from the LORD,
    who made heaven and earth.

He will not let your foot be moved;
    he who keeps you will not slumber.
He who keeps Israel
    will neither slumber nor sleep.

The LORD is your keeper;
    the LORD is your shade at your right hand.
The sun shall not strike you by day,
    nor the moon by night.

The LORD will keep you from all evil;
    he will keep your life.
The LORD will keep
    your going out and your coming in
    from this time on and forevermore.

Psalm 27

The LORD is my light and my salvation:
    whom shall I fear?
The LORD is the stronghold of my life;
    of whom shall I be afraid?

One thing I asked of the LORD,
    that will I seek after:
to live in the house of the LORD
    all the days of my life,
to behold the beauty of the LORD,
    and to inquire in his temple.

For he will hide me in his shelter
    in the day of trouble;
he will conceal me under the cover of his tent;
    he will set me high upon a rock.

Hear, O LORD, when I cry aloud,
    be gracious to me and answer me!
"Come," my heart says, "seek his face!"
    Your face, LORD, do I seek.
    Do not hide your face from me.

Do not turn your servant away in anger,
    you who have been my help.
Do not cast me off, do not forsake me,
    O God of my salvation!
If my father and mother forsake me,
    the LORD will take me up.

I believe that I shall see the goodness of the LORD
    in the land of the living.
Wait for the LORD;
    be strong, and let your heart take courage;
    wait for the LORD!

The Priestly Blessing

The Lord bless you and keep you;
    the Lord make his face to shine upon you and
        be gracious to you;
    the Lord lift up his countenance upon you, and give
        you peace. (Num 6:24–26)

K'riat Sh'ma

The LORD is our God, the LORD alone. You shall love the LORD
your God with all your heart, and with all your soul, and with all
your might. Keep these words that I am commanding you today
in your heart. Recite them to your children and talk about them
when you are at home and when you are away, when you lie
down and when you rise. Bind them as a sign on your hand, fix
them as an emblem on your forehead, and write them on the
doorposts of your house and on your gates. (Deut 6:4–9)

We Are Loved by an Unending Love

We are loved by an unending love.
We are embraced by arms that find us
    even when we are hidden from ourselves.
We are touched by fingers that soothe us
    even when we are too proud for soothing.
We are counseled by voices that guide us
    even when we are too embittered to hear.
We are loved by an everlasting love.

We are embraced by hands that uplift us
    even in the midst of a fall.
We are urged on by eyes that meet us
    even when we are too weak for meeting.
We are loved by an unending love.

Embraced, touched, soothed, and counseled,
    ours are the arms, the fingers, the voices;
    ours are the hands, the eyes, the smiles;
We are loved by an unending love.
                                —*Rabbi Rami Shapiro*

May You Live to See Your World Fulfilled

May you live to see your world fulfilled.
May your destiny be for worlds still to come.
May you trust in generations past and yet to be.
May your eyes shine with the light of holy words
And your face reflect the brightness of the heavens.
May your lips ever speak wisdom,
Your fulfillment be in justice
Even as you ever yearn to listen to the words of
The Holy Ancient One of old.

May your heart be filled with intuition
And your words be filled with insight.
May songs of praise be upon your tongue,
Your vision straight before you,
Even as you ever yearn to listen to the words of
The Holy Ancient One of old.[1]

Now It Is Time

Lord of All,
    we stand in awe before you,
    impelled by the visions of the harmony of all people.
We are children of many traditions,
    inheritors of shared wisdom and tragic
       misunderstandings,
    of proud hopes and humble successes.
Now it is time for us to meet
    in memory and truth,
    in courage and trust,
    in love and promise.[2]

CHRISTIANITY

Our Father

Our Father, who art in heaven, hallowed be thy name.
Thy kingdom come. Thy will be done, on earth as it is
   in heaven.
Give us this day our daily bread,
and forgive us our trespasses, as we forgive those
   who trespass against us.
And lead us not into temptation, but deliver us from evil,
   for Thine is the kingdom, the power, and the glory, for
   ever and ever.
Amen.

The Beatitudes

Blessed are the poor in spirit, for theirs is the kingdom of
   heaven.
Blessed are those who mourn, for they will be comforted.
Blessed are the meek, for they will inherit the earth.
Blessed are those who hunger and thirst for righteousness,
   for they will be filled.
Blessed are the merciful, for they will receive mercy.
Blessed are the pure in heart, for they will see God.
Blessed are the peacemakers, for they will be called
   children of God.
Blessed are those who are persecuted for righteousness'
   sake, for theirs is the kingdom of heaven.

(Matt 5:3–10)

The Magnificat

My soul magnifies the Lord, and my spirit rejoices in God
    my Savior,
      for he has looked with favor on the lowliness of his
        servant.
Surely, from now on all generations will call me blessed;
     for the Mighty One has done great things for me,
     and holy is his name.
His Mercy is for those who fear him from generation to
    generation.
He has shown strength with his arm;
     he has scattered the proud in the thoughts of their
       hearts.
He has brought down the powerful from their thrones,
     and lifted up the lowly;
     he has filled the hungry with good things,
     and sent the rich away empty.
He has helped his servant Israel, in remembrance of his
    mercy,
     according to the promise he made to our ancestors,
     to Abraham and to his descendants forever.

(Luke 1:47–55)

Peace Prayer

Lord, make me an instrument of Thy peace.
Where there is hatred, let me sow love.
Where there is injury, pardon.
Where there is doubt, faith.
Where there is despair, hope.
Where there is darkness, light.
Where there is sadness, joy.

O Divine Master, grant that I may not so much seek
    to be consoled, as to console;
    to be understood, as to understand;
    to be loved, as to love.
For it is in giving that we receive,
    it is in pardoning that we are pardoned,
    and it is in dying that we are born to eternal life.

—St. Francis of Assisi

Canticle to the Creatures

Most high, all-powerful, all good Lord!
All praise is yours, all glory, all honor, and all blessing.
To you alone, Most High, do they belong.
No mortal lips are worthy to pronounce your name.
All praise be yours, my Lord, through all that you have
    made.
And first, my Lord, brother Sun,
    who brings the day; and light you give us through him.
How beautiful is he, how radiant in all his splendor!
Of you, Most High, he bears the likeness.
All praise be yours, my Lord, through Sister Moon and
    Stars;
    in the heavens you have them, bright and precious
    and fair.
All praise be yours, My Lord, through Brothers Wind
    and Air,
    and fair and stormy, all the weather's moods,
    by which you cherish all that you have made.
All praise be yours, my Lord, through Sister Water,
    so useful, lowly, precious, and pure.
All praise be yours, my Lord, through Brother Fire,
    through whom you brighten up the night.

How beautiful he is, how gay! Full of power and strength.
All praise be yours, my Lord, through Sister Earth, our
     mother,
   who feeds us in her sovereignty and produces
   various fruits and colored flowers and herbs.
All praise be yours, my Lord, through those who grant
     pardon
   for love of you; through those who endure sickness and
     trial.
Happy those who endure in peace;
   by you, Most High, they will be crowned....
Praise and bless my Lord, and give him thanks,
   and serve him with great humility.

—St. Francis of Assisi

Beyond All Names

By what name shall I call upon you,
Who are beyond all names?
You are beyond all; what name shall I give to you?
What hymn can sing your praises
   or what word tell of you?
No mind can probe your secret,
   no intelligence comprehends you.
All that is spoken proceeds from you,
   but you remain beyond the reach of speech.
All that is thought stems from you,
   but you are beyond the power of thoughts.
All things proclaim you,
   the mute and those with the power of speech.
All things celebrate you,
   the unconscious and those endowed with
     consciousness.

The longings of the universe,
   the groanings of creation,
   are turned toward you in silent prayer.
All who know to interpret the world you have created
   sing to you a hymn of praise.
All that subsists you uphold.
All that moves you draw.
You are the goal of all that is;
   you are one, O God.
You are all the things that are and you are none;
You are not the part and you are not the whole.
All names are given to you and none comprehends you.
How shall I name you, who are beyond all names?
                —*The Hymn of St. Gregory Nazianzen*

For All Affected by Injustice

O God, we pray for all those in our world who are
   suffering from injustice:
For those who are discriminated against because of their
   race, color, or religion;
For those imprisoned for working for the relief of
   oppression;
For those who are hounded for speaking the inconvenient
   truth;
For those tempted to violence as a cry against
   overwhelming hardship;
For those deprived of reasonable health and education;
For those suffering from hunger and famine;
For those too weak to help themselves and who have no
   one else to help them;
For the unemployed who cry out for work but do not find it.
We pray for anyone of our acquaintance who is personally
   affected by injustice. Forgive us, Lord, if we

unwittingly share in the conditions or in a system
that perpetuates injustice.
Show us how we can serve your children and make your
love practical by washing their feet.[3]

—*Mother Teresa of Calcutta*

ISLAM

Sura 1 - Fatiha

In the name of Allah, Most Gracious, Most Merciful.
Praise be to Allah,
The Cherisher and Sustainer of the Worlds;
Most Gracious, Most Merciful;
Master of the Day of Judgment.
Thee do we worship,
And Thine aid we seek,
Show us the straight way,
The way of those on whom
Thou hast bestowed Thy Grace,
Those whose (portion)
Is not wrath,
And who go not astray.

Litany of the Ninety-Nine Names of God

You are the Merciful
You are the Compassionate
You are the King
You are the Holy one
You are the Fount of peace
You are the Protector of faith
You are the Guardian

You are the Incomparable
You are the Strongest
Response: Lord, hear us, have mercy upon us.

You are the Supreme
You are the Creator
You are the Bearer
You are the Fashioner
You are the Forgiving
You are the Dominating
You are the Giver of all Good
You are the Sustainer
You are the Solution
You are the Knowing
Response: Lord, hear us, have mercy upon us.

You are the Narrowing
You are the Broadening
You are the Humbling
You are the Exalting
You are the One Giving of power
You are the One Taking power away
You are the All-hearing
You are the All-seeing
You are the Arbiter
You are the Just
Response: Lord, hear us, have mercy upon us.

You are the Benevolent
You are the All-Cognizant
You are the Forbearing
You are the Elevated
You are the All-Forgiving
You are the Grateful
You are the Most High

You are the Greatest
You are the Preserver
You are the Provider
Response: Lord, hear us, have mercy upon us.

You are the One Calculator
You are the Sublime
You are the Generous
You are the Waiting
You are the Caring
You are the All Encompassing
You are the Wise
You are the Loving
You are the Glorious
You are the Raising to life
Response: Lord, hear us, have mercy upon us.

You are the Witness
You are the Truth
You are the Keeper
You are the Strong
You are the Firm
You are the Patron
You are the Praiseworthy
You are the Enumerating
You are the Maker
You are the Restorer
Response: Lord, hear us, have mercy upon us.

You are the Creator of life
You are the Creator of death
You are the Living
You are the Self-subsisting
You are the One without needs
You are the Glorified

You are the Unique
You are the Impenetrable
You are the Mighty
You are the All-Mighty
Response: Lord, hear us, have mercy upon us.

Sura 2: 255

Allah! There is no god but Him: the Living, the Eternal.
He neither slumbers nor sleeps. To Him belongs all that
    is in the heavens and the earth.
Who can intercede with Him without his permission?
He knows what is before them and what is behind
    them.
They cannot gain access to any thing out of His
    knowledge except what He pleases.
His throne is more vast than the heavens and the earth,
    and guarding of these both does not fatigue Him.
He is the Exalted, the Supreme.
O Allah! Give us steadfastness in obedience and keep us
    far from sin.
Give us sincerity in intention, and knowledge of that
    which is sacred.
Bestow on us guidance and constancy; seal our tongues
    with reason and wisdom.
Fill our hearts with knowledge and learning.
Keep us clean from within from what is forbidden
    and from those things of which we are uncertain.
Keep our hands from oppression and stealing.
Hide from our eyes immortality and treachery,
    and close our ears to foolish talk and calumny.
Grant this through Thy overflowing generosity and Thy
    mercy,
O merciful and Compassionate![4]

Muslim Daily Prayer

O God, you are peace.
From you comes peace, to you returns peace.
Revive us with a salutation of peace
    and lead us to your abode of peace.

HINDUISM

Hymn of Arjuna to the Supreme God in The Bhagavad Gita

Full just it is that in praise of Thee
The world should find its pleasure and its joy,
That monsters by terror [tamed] should scatter in all
    directions,
And that all who've won perfection should do Thee
    homage.
For why should they not revere Thee, great as is thy Self,
More to be prized art Thou than Brahma, [Thou] the first
    Creator,
God's Lord, the world's [abiding] home, unending,
Thou art Imperishable, Being, Not-Being and what
    surpasses both.
Thou art the Primal God, Primeval Person,
Thou of this universe the last proper and resting place,
Thou the knower and what is to be known, [Thou our]
    final home,
O Thou whose forms are infinite, by whom the whole
    [universe] was spun,
All hail [to Thee], when I stand before Thee,
[All hail] when I stand behind Thee,
All hail to Thee wherever I may be,
[All hail to Thee], Thou All![5]

Gayatri or Guru Mantra

O God, the Giver of Life,
Remover of pains and sorrows,
Bestower of happiness,
    and Creator of the universe:
Thou are most luminous, pure, and adorable.
We meditate on Thee.
May Thou inspire and guide our intellect in the right
    direction.[6]

Prayer from the Svetasvatara Upanishad

The whole universe is ever in his power.
He is pure consciousness, the creator of time:
    all-powerful, all-knowing.
It is under his rule that the work of creation revolves in
    its evolution,
    and we have earth, and water, and ether, and fire and air.
His being is the source of all being,
    the seed of all things that in this life have their life.
He is beyond time and space, and yet he is the God of
    infinite forms
    who dwells in our inmost thoughts and who is seen by
    those who love him.
May God who is hidden in nature,
    even as the silkworm is hidden in the web of silk he
    made,
    lead us to unison with his own Spirit.[7]

Prayer Adapted from the Upanishads

Lead me from death to life, from falsehood to truth.
Lead me from despair to hope, from fear to trust.
Lead me from hate to love, from war to peace.
Let peace fill our heart, our world, our universe.[8]

Vedic Peace Mantra

Om. May the circumstances of all beings be auspicious.
May all beings enjoy peace.
May all be full and may all prosper
    and be happy and free from disease.
May all strive to be kind to others.
May none despair.

Prayer from the Vedas

O God,
    let us be united.
Let us speak in harmony.
Let our minds apprehend alike.
Common be our prayer;
    common be the end of our assembly;
    common be our resolution;
    common be our deliberations.
Alike be our feelings.
Unified be our hearts.
Common be our intentions.
Perfect be our unity.[9]

Shanti Path—Hymn of Peace

May there be peace in the higher regions.
May there be peace in the firmament.
May there be peace on earth.
May the waters flow peacefully.
May the herbs and plants grow peacefully.
May all the living powers bring unto us peace.
The supreme Lord is peace.
May we all be in peace, peace, and only peace,
    and may that peace come unto each of us.
Shanti, shanti, shanti.[10]

BUDDHISM

(Prayers in the Theravada tradition, the school of Buddhism that draws its scriptural inspiration from the Tipitaka, or Pali canon.)

Protection

Many deities and men, yearning after good, have pondered on blessings. Pray, tell me the greatest blessing!

[The Buddha:]

Not to associate with the foolish, but to associate with the wise; and to honor those who are worthy of honor—this is the greatest blessing.

To reside in a suitable locality, to have done meritorious actions in the past and to set oneself in the right course—this is the greatest blessing.

To have much learning, to be skillful in handicraft, well-trained in discipline, and to be of good speech—this is the greatest blessing.

To support mother and father, to cherish wife and children, and to be engaged in peaceful occupation—this is the greatest blessing.

To be generous in giving, to be righteous in conduct, to help one's relatives, and to be blameless in action—this is the greatest blessing.

To loathe more evil and abstain from it, to refrain from intoxicants, and to be steadfast in virtue—this is the greatest blessing.

To be respectful, humble, contented, and grateful; and to listen to the Dhamma on due occasions—this is the greatest blessing.

To be patient and obedient, to associate with monks, and to have religious discussions on due occasions—this is the greatest blessing.

Self-restraint, a holy and chaste life, the perception of the Noble Truths and the realization of Nibbana—this is the greatest blessing.

A mind unruffled by the vagaries of fortune, from sorrow freed, from defilements cleansed, from fear liberated—this is the greatest blessing.

Those who thus abide, ever remain invincible, in happiness established. These are the greatest blessings.

—From the Maha-mangala Sutta in the Sutta-Nipata, v. 258ff[11]

A Buddhist Litany of Peace

As we are together, praying for peace, let us be truly with each other.

(Silence)

Let us be at peace within ourselves, our bodies and our minds, our emotions, and our spirit.

(*Silence*)

Let us return to ourselves and become wholly ourselves.

(*Silence*)

Let us be aware of the source of being common to us all and to all living things.

(*Silence*)

Evoking the presence of the Great Compassion, let us open our hearts to receive compassion—for ourselves and for all living beings.

(*Silence*)

Let us pray that all living beings may realize that they are all brothers and sisters, all nourished from the same source of life.

(*Silence*)

Let us pray that we ourselves may cease to be the cause of suffering to each other.

(*Silence*)

Let us pledge ourselves to live in a way which will not deprive other beings of air, water, food, shelter, or the chance to live.

(*Silence*)

With humility, with awareness of the uniqueness of life, and with compassion for the suffering around us, let us pray for the establishment of peace in our hearts and peace on earth.[12]

The Buddha's Words on Loving Kindness

This is what should be done
By one who is skilled in goodness,
And who knows the path of peace:

Let them be able and upright,
Straightforward and gentle in speech,
Humble and not conceited,
Contented and easily satisfied,
Unburdened with duties and frugal in their ways.
Peaceful and calm and wise and skillful,
Not proud or demanding in nature....
Let none deceive another,
Or despise any being in any state.
Let none through anger or ill-will
Wish harm upon another.
Even as a mother protects with her life
Her child, her only child,
So with a boundless heart
Should one cherish all living beings;
Radiating kindness over the entire world:
Spreading upwards to the skies,
And downwards to the depths;
Outwards and unbounded,
Freed from hatred and ill-will.
Whether standing or walking, seated or lying down,
Free from drowsiness,
One should sustain this recollection.
This is said to be the sublime abiding.
                    —*From the Karaniya Metta Sutta*[13]

The Noble Eightfold Path

The Way to the End of Suffering:
Right view
Right intentions
Right speech
Right action
Right livelihood

Right effort
Right mindfulness
Right concentration[14]

Prayer in Mahayana Buddhism

Prayer for Mahayana Buddhists includes reciting mantras, singing "hymn-like" praises of Buddhas and Bodhisattvas (people dedicated to attaining Enlightenment), chanting sacred names, and reciting sutras either from texts or from memory, and performance of daily liturgical ceremonies. Praises can be supplication of a deity, such as Amitabha Buddha or Avalokiteshvara Bodhisattva, or chanting names of Dharma-methods, such as the Vows of a Bodhisattva. An example of each[15]:

Namo A Mi Tuo Fuo (Namo Amitabha)
(I return to and rely on the Buddha of Limitless Light.)

Namo Guan Shi Yin Pu Sa
(I return to and rely on the Awakened Being Who Hears the Voices of All in the World.)

Four Vast Vows of All Bodhisattvas

Living beings are boundless; even so, I vow to save them all.
Afflictions are endless; even so, I vow to cut them all off.
Methods of practice are measureless, even so, I vow to learn them all.
The Buddha's way is supreme; even so, I vow to realize it.

SIKHISM

A Sikh Prayer

In the beginning God brought forth his light,
    from his creative power came all beings.
From the One Light the entire universe came forth.
So who is good and who is bad?
Stray not in doubt, O Siblings of Destiny!
The Creator is in the creation,
    the creation is in the Creator,
He is ever-present, pervading everywhere.
The clay is the same, while it is fashioned
    into many forms by the Master Potter.
There is no fault with the vessel of clay,
    as there is no fault with the Potter.
Within all is the One True Lord.
It is by His will that all exist.
One who realizes God's will comes to know God.
He is the true servant of the Lord.
The invisible Lord cannot be seen.
The Guru has blessed me with this sweet realization.
I see the Perfect Pure Lord everywhere.

(Aval Allah[16]*)*

All Nature Is Yours

Nature we see
Nature we hear
Nature we observe with awe, wonder and joy
Nature in the skies
Nature in the whole creation
Nature in the sacred texts

Nature in all reflection
Nature in food, in water, in clothes, and in love for all
Nature in species, kinds and colors
Nature in life-forms
Nature in good deeds
Nature in pride and ego
Nature in air, water and fire
Nature in the soil of the earth
All nature is yours, O powerful Creator
You command it, observe, and pervade it.

(Adi Granth[17])

Awake in peace, sit in peace.
Understand this message,
leave fear and be serene.
The Savior is our one Lord.
Sleep without fear, awake without fear.
Everywhere you are present, O Lord.
Peace at home and peace outdoors.

(Adi Granth[18])

In the company of saints and holy people
Yours and mine are no more.
Only Thine, O Lord.
No one an enemy, none a stranger.
As friends we got on with each other.
What the Lord wills is good.
This wisdom is received in blessing from saints.
The One Lord with us all.

(Adi Granth[19])

BAHA'I

A Baha'i Prayer for Unity

O my God! O my God!
Verily I invoke thee and supplicate before thy threshold,
  asking thee that all thy mercies may descend upon
    these souls.
Bless them with your favor and your truth.

O Lord! Unite and bind together our hearts,
  join in accord all our souls,
    and exhilarate our spirits through the signs of thy
      sanctity and oneness.
O Lord! Make these faces radiant through the light of thy
    oneness.
Strengthen the loins of thy servants in the service of thy
    kingdom.

O Lord, thou possessor of infinite mercy!
O Lord of forgiveness and pardon!
Forgive our sins, pardon our shortcomings,
  and cause us to turn to the kingdom of thy clemency,
  invoking the kingdom of might and power,
  humble at thy shrine and submissive before thy glory.

O Lord God! Make us as waves of the sea,
  as flowers of the garden, united,
  agreed through the bounties of thy love.
O Lord! Open our hearts through the signs of your
    oneness,
  and make all humankind as stars shining
  from the same height of glory,
  as peaceful fruits growing upon the tree of life.

Verily, thou art the Almighty, the Self-Subsistent, the Giver,
    the Forgiving, the Pardoner, the Omniscient, the one
    Creator.

                             —'Abdu'l-Baha[20]

Do not be satisfied until each one with whom you are
    concerned
  is to you like a member of your family.
Regard each one either as a father, a brother,
  or as a sister, a mother, or a child.
If you can attain to this,
  your difficulties will vanish.
You will know what to do.

                             —'Abdu'l-Baha[21]

In the estimation of God, all people are equal.
There is no distinction or preference for any soul
  in the realm of His justice and equity.
God did not make these divisions.
They have their origin in humankind.
Therefore, as they are against the plan and purpose of God,
  they are false and imaginary.
This variety in forms and coloring,
  manifest in all the kingdoms,
  is according to creative wisdom and divine purpose.
The diversity in the human family should be the cause
  of love and harmony, as it is in music
  where the different notes blend together
  in the making of a perfect chord.

                             —'Abdu'l-Baha[22]

NATIVE AMERICAN

An Indian Prayer

O Great Spirit, whose voice I hear in the winds
    and whose breath gives life to all the world: hear me!
I am small and weak; I need your strength and wisdom.
Let me walk in beauty and make my eyes
    ever behold the red and purple sunset.
Make my hands respect the things you have made
    and my ears sharp to hear your voice.
Make me wise so that I may understand the things
You have taught my people.
Let me learn the lessons you have hidden
    in every leaf and rock.
I seek strength, not to be greater than my brother,
    but to fight my greatest enemy—myself.
Make me always ready to come to you
    with clean hands and straight eyes.
So when life fades, as the fading sunset,
    my spirit may come to you without shame.[23]

Ojibway Prayer

Grandfather,
Look at our brokenness.
We know that in all creation
    only the human family has strayed from the Sacred Way.
We know that we are the ones who are divided
    and we are the ones who must come back together
    to walk the Sacred Way.
Grandfather, Sacred One,

Teach us love, compassion and honor,
    that we may heal the earth
    and heal each other.
Creator, Earth Mother, we thank you for our lives
    and this beautiful day.
Thank you for the bright sun
    and the rain we received last night.
Thank you for this circle of friends
    and the opportunity to be together.
We thank you especially at this time
    for the giveaway of their lives made by
    the chickens, beets, carrots, grains and lettuce.
We thank them for giving of their lives so we may
    continue our lives through this great blessing.
Please help us honor them through how we live our
      lives.[24]

Sioux Prayer

Grandfather, Great Spirit, all over the world
    the faces of living things are alike.
With tenderness, they have come up out of the ground.
Look upon your children that they may face the winds
    and walk the good road to the day of quiet.
Grandfather, Great Spirit, fill us with the light.
Give us the strength to understand and the eyes to see.
Teach us to walk the soft earth as relatives to all that live.[25]

Notes

Introduction

1. Findings of an Exploratory Consultation on Interreligious Prayer: Final Statement (Bangalore, India, 1996), in *Pro Dialogo*, 98 (1998/2), 231.

2. Ibid., 236.

3. *"Declaration of the Relationship of the Church to Non-Christian Religions (Nostra Aetate),"* The Documents of Vatican II (America Press, 1966), 660, art. 1.

4. CBIC Commission for Dialogue and Ecumenism, "Guidelines for Interreligious Dialogue," 2nd rev. ed. (New Delhi: CBCI Centre, 1989), 68, par. 82.

5. S. Wesley Ariarajah, *Not Without My Neighbour* (Geneva: WCC Publications, 1999), 56.

Chapter 1

1. J. Russel Chandran, "Theological Assessment of Interreligious Prayer," in *Pro Dialogo*, 98 (1998/2), 201.

2. Franco Sottocornola, "Biblical Perspectives on Interreligious Prayer," in *Pro Dialogo*, 98 (1998/2), 180.

3. "Theological Reflections on Interreligious Prayer: Final Statement (Bose, Italy, 1997)," in *Pro Dialogo*, 98 (1998/2), 238, 239.

4. Chandran, "Theological Assessment," 201, 202.

5. Ibid., 202.

6. Sottocornola, "Biblical Perspectives on Interreligious Prayer," 167, 170.

7. Ibid., 169.

8. Ibid., 178, 179. This reading of the "history of salva-tion" through "four covenants" goes back at least to the second century church father Irenaeus, in *Adversus Haereses*, 3, 11, 8.

9. Ibid., 179.

10. Kevin Godfrey, "Hospitality," in *The New Dictionary of Catholic Spirituality* (Collegeville, MN: The Liturgical Press, 1993), 515, 516.

11. Pierre F. de Béthune, "The Bond of Peace: Theological Reflections About Interreligious Prayer," in *Pro Dialogo*, 98 (1998/2), 161.

12. "Theological Reflections on Interreligious Prayer: Final Statement," 237, 238.

13. Ibid., 240.

Chapter 2

1. Wesley Ariarajah, "Can We Pray Together? Inter-religious Prayer: A Protestant Perspective," in *Pro Dialogo*, 98 (1998/2), 262.

2. *Apophatic* comes from the Greek *apophasis*, the way of negation or denial. The apophatic way of praying in the Christian tradition is the way of negation. It says that since no thoughts, images, ideas, words, or symbols can express God's innermost reality, we must in the end enter the darkness in love.

3. Joseph Cardinal Ratzinger, *Truth and Tolerance: Chris-tian Belief and World Religions* (San Francisco, CA: Ignatius Press, 2004), 103, 104, 106.

4. John Paul II, "To Representatives of Various Religions on the World Day of Prayer for Peace," in *Interreligious Dialogue:*

The Official Teaching of the Catholic Church (1963–1995), ed. Francesco Gioia (Boston: Pauline, 1994), par. 1, 2, 3, 4, nos. 534–537, 343, 344. Also: http://www.vatican.va/holy_father/ john_paul_ii/speeches/1986/october/documents/hf_jp-ii_spe_ 19861027_prayer-peace-assisi_en.html

5. John Paul II, "To the Roman Curia (December 22, 1986)," in *Interreligious Dialogue,* ed. Francesco Gioia, par. 3, nos. 564, 361.

6. Ibid.

7. *Pastoral Constitution on the Church in the Modern World (Gaudium et Spes),* December 7, 1965, no. 22. See also *Dogmatic Constitution on the Church (Lumen Gentium),* November 21, 1964, no. 16.

8. John Paul II, *The Lord and Giver of Life (Dominum et Vivificantem),* May 18, 1986, no. 53.

9. John Paul II, *The Mission of the Redeemer (Redemptoris Missio),* December 7, 1990, no. 28.

10. Ibid., no. 11.

11. John Paul II, *Redeemer of Humankind (Redemptor Hominis),* March 4, 1979, no. 6.

12. Gavin D'Costa, "Theological Reflections on Interreligious Prayer: The Catholic Tradition," in *Pro Dialogo,* 98 (1998/2), 255.

13. Ariarajah, *Not Without My Neighbour,* 38.

14. Joseph Cardinal Ratzinger, *Truth and Tolerance,* 105.

15. *Interreligious Dialogue,* par.13, nos. 820, 570.

16. "Dialogue and Proclamation," in *Interreligious Dialogue,* par. 49, nos. 973, 625.

17. "Theological Reflections: Final Statement," 239, 241.

18. D'Costa, "Theological Reflections," 257.

19. Ariarajah, *Not Without My Neighbour,* 38.

20. Ibid., 39.

Chapter 3

1. John Paul II, "To Representatives of Various Religions," par. 3.

2. In July 1996 and April 2002, about fifty Buddhist and Christian monks and nuns came together for historic, five-day encounters at Gethsemani Abbey, Kentucky. For more details, see www.monasticdialog.com.

3. John Paul II, "To Representatives of Various Religions," par. 3.

4. Sottocornola, "Biblical Perspectives on Interreligious Prayer," 171, 172.

5. Ibid., 185.

6. Ratzinger, *Truth and Tolerance,* 108, 109.

7. Jacques Dupuis, *Christianity and the Religions* (New York: Orbis Books, 2002), 243.

8. Ibid., 238, 248.

9. Maurice Borrmans, *Guidelines for Dialogue between Christians and Muslims,* translated by R. Marston Speight (New York/Mahwah, NJ: Paulist Press, 1990), 107–109.

10. Papal Address to Turkey's Religious Affairs Director, "We Belong to the Family of Those Who Believe in the One God," Ankara, Turkey, Nov. 28, 2006.

11. Dupuis, *Christianity and the Religions,* 249.

12. Ibid., 250.

13. *The Psalms of David: Universal Prayers of Praise and Thanksgiving,* selected by Muhammad Abdul-Rauf, Rabbi Walter S. Wurzburger, and Albert C. Outler (Dallas, TX: Center for World Thanksgiving, ND).

14. Thomas Thangaraj, "A Theological Reflection on the Experience of Interreligious Prayer," in *Pro Dialogo,* 98 (1998/2),191,192.

15. "Theological Reflections on Interreligious Prayer," 235.

16. D'Costa, "Theological Reflections," 257.

Chapter 4

1. "Theological Reflections on Interreligious Prayer," 239.

2. I am indebted, for the category schema in the remainder of this chapter, to *All in Good Faith: A Resource Book for Multi-Faith Prayer,* Jean Potter and Marcus Braybrooke, eds. (The World Congress of Faiths: Great Britain, 1997), 69, 70.

Chapter 5

1. Chandran, "Theological Assessment of Interreligious Prayer," 205.

2. Ibid., 206.

3. Tosh Araj and Wesley Ariarajah, eds. *Spirituality in Interfaith Dialogue* (Geneva: WCC Publications, 1989), 1, 2.

4. Benedict XVI, *God Is Love (Deus Caritas Est),* December 25, 2005, no. 31c.

5. Sottocornola, "Biblical Perspectives on Interreligious Prayer," 184.

6. Ibid.

Chapter 6: Appendix

1. *Babylonian Talmud,* Berachot 17a, Lawrence Kushner, trans., in *Twelve Jewish Steps to Recovery* (Woodstock, VT: Jewish Lights Publishing, 1991), 111.

2. *Forms of Prayer for Jewish Worship* (Reform Synagogues of Great Britain, 1977), 316.

3. From *All in Good Faith: A Resource Book for Multi-Faith Prayer,* Jean Potter and Marcus Braybrooke, eds. (The World Congress of Faiths: Great Britain, 1997), 79. This excellent resource contains a series of articles on prayer in the world religions from the viewpoints of representatives of the different reli-

gions; an anthology of readings and prayers organized around various themes; and examples of nine different services of interreligious prayer.

4. Ibid., 98.

5. *Hindu Scriptures,* ed. R. C. Zaehner (London: Dent, 1966), 298.

6. Potter and Braybrooke, *All in Good Faith,* 109.

7. Ibid., 85.

8. Ibid., 121.

9. Ibid., 73.

10. Ibid., 88.

11. From *Everyman's Ethics: Four Discourses by the Buddha (WH 14),* translated by Narada Thera (Kandy: Buddhist Publication Society, 1985). See also http://www.accesstoinsight. org/tipitaka/kn/snp/snp.2.04.nara.html

12. Potter and Braybrooke, *All in Good Faith,* 108, 109.

13. From *Chanting Book: Morning and Evening Puja and Reflections,* translated from the Pali by The Amaravati Sangha (Hemel Hempstead: Amaravati Publications, 1994). See also http://www.accesstoinsight.org/tipitaka/kn/khp/khp.9.amar.html

14. From *The Wheel,* translation by Bhikku Bodhi, Publication No. 308/311 (Kandy: Buddhist Publication Society, revised edition, 1994). See also http://www.accesstoinsight.org/lib/authors/bodhi/waytoend.html

15. These examples are drawn from the *City of 10,000 Buddhas Recitation Handbook,* Burlingame, CA: Buddhist Text Translation Society, 2005.

16. Potter and Braybooke, *All in Good Faith,* 108.

17. Ibid., 84.

18. Ibid., 87.

19. Ibid., 94.

20. Ibid., 126.

21. Ibid., 89.

22. Ibid., 93.

23. Mary Ann Walt, Joanne Church, et al., *Worship and Educational Resources from American Indians* (Minnesota Indian Ecumenical Ministries: Minnesota Council of Churches, 2003), 36.

24. Ibid.

25. Ibid.